First Biographies

Maurice Sendak

by Eric Braun

Consulting Editor: Gail Saunders-Smith, PhD

Capstone
press
Mankato, Minnesota

Pebble Books are published by Capstone Press,
151 Good Counsel Drive, P.O. Box 669, Mankato, Minnesota 56002.
www.capstonepress.com

1 2 3 4 5 6 10 09 08 07 06 05

Library of Congress Cataloging-in-Publication Data
Braun, Eric, 1971–
    Maurice Sendak / by Eric Braun.
    p. cm.—(First biographies)
    Includes bibliographical references and index.
    ISBN 0-7368-3640-3 (hardcover)
    ISBN 0-7368-5092-9 (paperback)
    1. Sendak, Maurice—Juvenile literature. 2. Authors, American—20th century—
Biography—Juvenile literature. 3. Illustrators—United States—Biography—Juvenile
literature. 4. Children's stories—Authorship—Juvenile literature. I. Title. II. First
biographies (Mankato, Minn.)
PS3569.E6Z597 2005
741.6'42'092—dc22   2004013302

Summary: Simple text and photographs present the life of Maurice Sendak.

Note to Parents and Teachers

The First Biographies set supports national history standards for units on people and culture. This book describes and illustrates the life of Maurice Sendak. The images support early readers in understanding the text. The repetition of words and phrases helps early readers learn new words. This book also introduces early readers to subject-specific vocabulary words, which are defined in the Glossary section. Early readers may need assistance to read some words and to use the Table of Contents, Glossary, Read More, Internet Sites, and Index sections of the book.

Table of Contents

Time Line

1928
born

Young Maurice

In 1928, Maurice Sendak was born in Brooklyn, New York. When he was a young boy, his dad read him bedtime stories.

Brooklyn, New York, in 1928; Maurice as an adult (inset)

Time Line

1928
born

Maurice was often sick when he was growing up. He would look out the window and watch kids playing. Maurice drew pictures of them.

Time Line

1928
born

1946
graduates from
high school

In high school, Maurice
drew his own comic strip.
He later drew pictures
for a science book.
He went to art school
to learn more.

the art school Maurice went to in New York City

Time Line

1928 born	**1946** graduates from high school	**1948** works at toy store

Beginning Artist

In 1948, Maurice
worked at a toy store.
He helped make displays
for the store's windows.
At night, he painted and
studied children's books.

◀ one of the current FAO Schwarz toy stores, the toy
store chain where Maurice worked after high school

Time Line

1928	1946	1948
born	graduates from high school	works at toy store

In 1951, Maurice illustrated his first book called *The Wonderful Farm.* Children enjoy reading this story about two girls and many talking animals.

1951
illustrates
first book

Time Line

1928
born

1946
graduates from
high school

1948
works at
toy store

Illustrator and Author

In 1956, he wrote and illustrated *Kenny's Window*. In this book, a boy answers questions from a dream. He talks to animals and toys.

◀ Maurice working on an illustration

1951
illustrates
first book

Time Line

1928 born	**1946** graduates from high school	**1948** works at toy store

His most famous book
is called *Where the Wild
Things Are.* Many children
love this book about
scary creatures.

◀ Maurice standing in front of an illustration from
Where the Wild Things Are

1951
illustrates
first book

Time Line

1928 born	**1946** graduates from high school	**1948** works at toy store

Maurice won a Caldecott Medal for *Where the Wild Things Are* in 1964. This award honors the best children's book illustrator each year.

◀ Maurice standing by an illustration from *Where the Wild Things Are*

1951
illustrates
first book

1964
wins Caldecott Medal for
Where the Wild Things Are

Time Line

1928	1946	1948
born	graduates from high school	works at toy store

Maurice has illustrated
almost 100 books.
His books are some
of the most popular
children's books ever.

1951
illustrates
first book

1964
wins Caldecott Medal for
Where the Wild Things Are

Glossary

Caldecott Medal—an award given each year to the best children's book illustrator; the winner must be someone who lives in the United States.

comic strip—a story told using panels of cartoons; many newspapers print comic strips.

famous—well known to many people

illustrate—to draw pictures for a book or other publication

popular—liked or enjoyed by many people

Read More

Gaines, Ann. *Maurice Sendak.* A Real-Life Reader Biography. Bear, Del.: Mitchell Lane Publishers, 2002.

Woods, Mae. *Maurice Sendak.* Children's Authors. Minneapolis: Abdo, 2000.

Internet Sites

FactHound offers a safe, fun way to find Internet sites related to this book. All of the sites on FactHound have been researched by our staff.

Here's how:

1. Visit *www.facthound.com*
2. Type in this special code **0736836403** for age-appropriate sites. Or enter a search word related to this book for a more general search.
3. Click on the **Fetch It** button.

FactHound will fetch the best sites for you!

Index

Word Count: 201
Grade: 1
Early-Intervention Level: 16

Editorial Credits
Mari C. Schuh, editor; Heather Kindseth, set designer; Patrick D. Dentinger, book designer; Kelly Garvin, photo researcher; Scott Thoms, photo editor

Photo Credits
AP/Wide World Photos, 14; Capstone Press/Karon Dubke, 12; Corbis/Bettmann, 4, 6; Corbis Sygma/Ellis Richard, 20; Getty Images Inc./Mario Tama, 10; Getty Images Inc./Spencer Platt, 1; Getty Images Inc./Time Life Pictures, 18; Globe Photos/Mike Wells, 4 (inset); Globe Photos/Tricia Meadows, cover; The Image Works/Topham, 16; Photo courtesy of Cornelia Seckel, Publisher of "The Art Students League of New York: A History" by Raymond J. Steiner and Art Times, a monthly literary journal and resource for the fine and performing arts, 8